Steam Memories On Shed: 1950's - 19

No. 94 SCOTTISH REGION EN
& Their Motive Power

THE 60 GROUP: 60A to 60E

David Dunn

Copyright Book Law Publications 2017
ISBN 978-1-909625-70-9

INTRODUCTION

In this album we feature those engine sheds formerly belonging to the Highland Railway which gained BR shed codes at Nationalisation – sheds 60A to 60E and their sub sheds which became BR property. Many of the sheds were built of stone but most of the smaller buildings survived into BR even though their construction included mainly wood – the Highland it seems could not afford longevity!

The motive power on offer does not include any of the glamorous 'namers' of the Big Four but there are a couple of the less well known examples which plied these parts daily without turning heads. Big ones and little ones, but mainly medium sized ones fill these pages; nearly all of them were ancient when BR inherited them but they managed to keep going with care and maintenance.

Except for Inverness, not much in the way of modernisation was lavished on these scattered depots and that will become apparent as the images unfold. Therefore the locations remained virtually untouched from how they were first put into operation. Nevertheless, we have hopefully gathered a nice bunch of images which will convey what the engine sheds and motive power of the former HR appeared like under British Railways. Thanks to The Armstrong Railway Photographic Trust and to Michael Halbert for the use of their material.

David Dunn, Cramlington 2017

(cover) See page 27.

(previous page) This is Boat of Garten – a sub of Aviemore – with the former Great North of Scotland Railway 4-4-0 No.62275 SIR DAVID STEWART of LNER Class D40. The undated image was captured circa summer 1953 during the last year that the tender carried the BR wording and the locomotive carried a brass nameplate. At its next shopping in January and February 1954, the nameplate was removed and a painted version of the name (in the parsimonious style of the North British, and the Highland) was applied. No.62275 had been a Keith engine from 31st August 1952 and would have become a regular at Boat of Garten. The 4-4-0 was condemned during the third week of December 1955. You can tell it's a summers' morning as the enginemen are in tee-shirts and the sky is threatening. Note also the new and recently fitted heating hose. *J.D. Mills, M. Halbert coll.*

Printed and bound by The Amadeus Press, Cleckheaton, West Yorkshire
First published in the United Kingdom by Book Law Publications, 382 Carlton Hill, Nottingham, NG4 1JA

Pickersgill Caledonian Railway 3P 4-4-0 No.54463 was typical of the pre-Group passenger types allocated to Inverness during BR days. Eight or nine of these useful 4-4-0s served 60A for much of the 1940s and 50s' and those few years (months more-like) of the 60s' before steam was banished.
L. Turnbull (ARPT).

(opposite) Time to look at what the Highland Railway passed on to BR. This 4-6-0 was classified 5F (5MT by BR) and was built to the design of C. Cumming. No.57956 was one of eight such engines constructed between 1917 and 1919 and numbered in the HR 75 to 82. Our subject was No.81. All eight became LMS engines numbered 17950 to 17957 but only five of those survived to get these BR numbers withdrawals starting in 1946: 57950, 57951, 57954, 57955, and 57956. The last of them, No.57954, succumbed in October 1952. Our subject had been condemned during the previous May. Latterly (since March 1944) all of them were allocated to Inverness but pre-war allocations included two at Kyle of Lochalsh in July 1935, with another pair at Dingwall; Inverness looked after the other four. Deceptively to the eye perhaps, these locomotives only weighed fifty-six and a half tons, without tender of course, which appears rather low compared to the 72-tons of a Stanier Class 5 for instance. *(top & bottom)* Awaiting its go on the turntable, Tuesday 24th April 1951 and then reversing into a stall on that same Tuesday. The LMS lettering remained on the tender to the scrapyard. *both C.J.B. Sanderson (ARPT).*

(above) Another Cumming design was the 'Clan' class 4-6-0 classified 4P of which eight were put into traffic between 1919 and 1921. All of them carried names – applied with paint in the dubious Scottish tradition – of famous Clans and were numbered 49, 51, 52, 53, 54, 55, 56, 57 (No.50 had been taken up by a 'Castle' beforehand). The LMS were sensible enough to place the class in one number group – 14762 to 14769 – but only one of them, our subject here, survived to carry the BR number 54767. CLAN MACKINNON and sister No.14764 CLAN MUNRO were the only HR 'Clans' to survive Nationalisation when both were allocated to Aviemore (No.14764 survived by just days and was withdrawn in January 1948, being cut up at Inverness). No.54767 went in January 1950 and was cut up during the following March at Kilmarnock works. Pre-war all of the class except No.14766 at Inverness, were to be found in different areas of the old Caledonian system; in 1935 for instance four of them were allocated to Balornock shed in Glasgow, two were at Stirling and No.14764 was shedded at Oban. No.14759 was the first of the class to be withdrawn, a deed carried out in 1944. Wartime found six of the class at Inverness in 1944 whilst Nos.14758 and 14760 were working from the former South Western' shed at Ayr. Note the ash plant on the left with the open wagon standing beneath the hoist ready to accept the contents of the ash skip; yet another of those dirty jobs associated with steam locomotives. *K.H. Cockerill (ARPT).*

(opposite) Resident ex-CR 3P No.54487 ready for work on 1st August 1957.

D. Fairley (ARPT).

Ex-HR Cumming 4-6-0 No.57955 sits comfortably on the turntable on Tuesday 3rd June 1952. By this period St Rollox works was sending out locomotives with the large size cab side numbers whereas these are the smaller (normal) size to fit the location which is a bit cramped with that tablet catcher in situ. At least the BR emblem has been applied to the tender but this 4F was coming very rapidly to the end of its life and in July it was withdrawn and sent away to Kilmarnock for scrapping, the penultimate member of the class.   *I.S.Jones (ARPT).*

8   The two Inverness 'Pugs' Nos.56011 and 56038 take in the last of the sunshine during an August evening in 1957.   *L. Turnbull (ARPT)*.

An elevated, but undated view of 60A and its surroundings; this must be towards the end or at least late 1950s judging from the motor vehicles (and no I'm not going to name them to show my age but is that rear Ford a Zephyr or a Zodiac?). Looking at this place from another aspect, the locomotive depot must have been the largest polluter in Inverness if not the Highlands. Perhaps there were some political leanings taking place to rid the area of steam as soon as possible! The ash plant appears to have recently had a coat of paint (and my cynical mind thought it was only stations before closure that were treated to a lick of paint) so modellers take note; in this b&w image the paint appears to be a light grey. Are such appliances available in model form or is it still a case of scratch building?

J.W. Armstrong (ARPT).

It is Friday 29th July 1955, fairly late evening and with a clear sky. All the stalls in this segment of the roundhouse are full for the night; there isn't an LMS Standard design in sight, they are all pre-Group engines. Diesels are in their infancy and most haven't even been designed yet. The Modernisation Plan for BR was soon to become reality but in Northern Scotland it would have little effect straight away. Therefore at this moment in time the world was at peace, at least in this part of it. *F.W. Hampson (ARPT).*

The erstwhile HR 0-4-4T No.55053 inside Lochgorm locomotive works at Inverness in August 1957, nearly eight months after withdrawal. Besides the wheels, a few other items have been removed such as the all-important brass plates. Note the heating hose left in situ too. The front splasher on this side of the engine appears to have taken a bash during the parting of the wheels but otherwise the engine looks fairly fresh from its 1955 visit to St Rollox. This tank engine was the last of 173 locomotives inherited by the LMS from the HR. British Railways received twenty-nine of those, and all but two of them remained from 1953 when No.55053 and her sister No.55051 were active on the Dornoch branch. The latter 0-4-4T was withdrawn on 22nd June 1956 leaving our subject here to carry the flag for the Highland but catastrophe, in January 1957, whilst working the branch, rendered No.55053 incapable of carrying on and condemnation became inevitable (*see* page 53 for further information). The original class of these Drummond tank engines consisted four locomotives numbered 25, 40, 45, and 46, all built at Inverness during 1905-6. The LMS gave them the numbers 15051 to 15054 in the order of the HR numbering but 15052 was withdrawn in 1930, whilst 15054 followed in 1945 after complete closure of the Lybster branch. This left just 15051 and 15053 to become BR property and both had 40,000 added to their running numbers in 1949. The four tanks had been specifically built to work two branch lines which were in effect Light railways – the Dornoch branch and Lybster branch – which required low maximum axle loads of just below twelve tons. Their diminutive size will become quite apparent as more images of the two BR survivors are presented throughout this album. No.55053 was to only HR locomotive to receive the full BR lined black livery even the door was treated at the St Rollox repaint. *L. Turnbull (ARPT).*

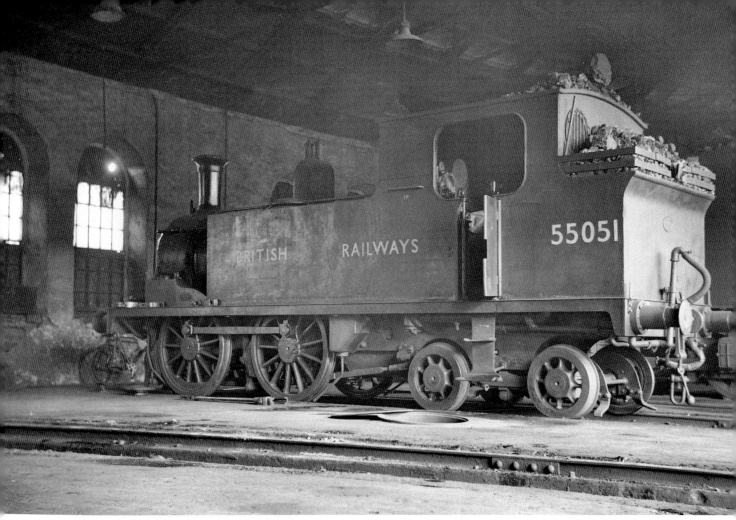

(above) No.55051 inside the Inverness roundhouse on an unknown date in the 1950s! The early BR livery was plain black but note the positioning of the figures virtually at the back end of the bunker side sheet; although looking lop-sided, there was a reason for the numbers being placed there. Note the cab door which opens outwards and its probable end position against the side sheet; the number is still readable (an image of this engine later on shows the door and number situation to full effect). The little wheels on the bogie are particularly noticeable and look more like accommodation bogies found in main works. The coaling process beneath the mechanical plant was not one of the better pieces of shed craft carried out by the 60A staff but bringing the engine onto the turntable and positioning the little tank in the roundhouse without dislodging that large lump of coal atop the cab roof defies description. *(opposite)* A broadside of No.55051 on the same day as the previous illustration; now that lump looks like some monstrous growth reaching for the sky! The Dornoch pair worked a fortnight about on the branch but each of them visited Inverness every four months or so for and heavy work to be carried out. Modellers note the 1P positioned exactly above the Y in railways. Plenty of roundhouse detail on view including the dirt and grime. But before we leave 55051, have a thought for the Lochgorm 1905 worksplate which sold at auction in July 2013 for £1,450!

both images S.C. Crook (ARPT).

No.56038 in 1958 with the H18 target board – its shunting duty number off shed? – looking more industrial than ever. This was to be the 'Pug's' last full year of operation as it was withdrawn in May 1959. Note one of the Barclay 0-4-0 diesel mechanical shunters hiding behind the saddletank. Four of these 204 h.p. diesels came new to Inverness in 1958 as follows: D2410 19th June, D2411 31st July, D2412 18th September, and D2413 8th October. It was to be November 1961 before any of the larger 350 h.p. 0-6-0 diesel-electric shunters arrived in the shape of D4095 and D4096 from Fort William of all places.

A.R. Thompson (ARPT).

The view from the other side of No.56038 on that same day in 1958 reveals sister No.56011 alongside. That 'Pug' would get the call to the scrapyard in December. Now it might be noted by some, but not by others, but I'll point it out anyway. In the last image part of the cab section of a Barclay diesel was just discernible. Coming round to this side of the locomotive, where the diesel would have shown even more of itself, the photographer has chosen to leave the diesel out of the frame. Such events were numerous amongst railway photographers, many of whom were in denial that the diesels ever existed – honestly. It is no doubt a massive missed opportunity to record a part of railway history that is still sparsely covered on film. However, one has to respect those photographers and thank them anyway for bringing us these wonderful images of the outgoing motive power, which still manage to brighten our lives.

A.R. Thompson (ARPT).

Long before the big cull of steam power, Inverness started storing redundant locomotives at the eastern end of the shed yard as witness 3P No.54480 complete with covered chimney on 16th May 1959. Of course, this 4-4-0 was one of Helmsdale's fleet. The ex-Caley engine was eventually withdrawn in August 1960 during the first cull, and ended up in the scrapyard of the BR works at Inverurie. *N.W. Skinner (ARPT).*

Retaining its original chimney, ex-CR 3F 0-6-0T No.56299 bathes in the evening sun light on Friday 3rd August 1956. This was the engine which took over from the LMS 3F No.47541, along with classmates Nos.56291 and 56301 which ousted the LMS 3Fs from Forres and Burghead sheds. No.56299 wasn't long for this world and was withdrawn in February 1957. The original stone-built arched entrances fronting each stall of the roundhouse was taken down in the 1940s when suitable supports had been erected to carry the massive roof. The design afforded some superb clutter free views of the roundhouse interior but more importantly it gave that much needed clearance – on personnel safety grounds – which had been a problem for decades.

F.W. Hampson (ARPT).

It's Pug No.56011's turn to share the limelight. Looking a little better than in previous images, the 0-4-0ST looks quite respectable in this 1st August 1957 view. Note the white painted coupling links.

D. Fairley (ARPT).

Something like ten years on from the image of No.55051 inside the roundhouse and the Inverness coaling gang have still not refined their bunker filling methods. This is one of the two Dornoch branch replacement engines from the Western Region, No.1646 inside the roundhouse on 14th June 1962 minus coupling rods. At this time steam had essentially finished in these parts and the roundhouse was inhabited by this Pannier, a Cl.3 2-6-2T No.40150 from Wick/Thurso, and an ex-CR 0-6-0 No.57587; all in the same state as this 0-6-0PT. The shed was cleared out soon afterwards but nobody had any idea what to do with this engine as it was still regarded as Western Region property. In and around the yards surrounding the depot a number of steam locomotives were stored pending reallocation or withdrawal; a proper clear-out had taken place. *F.W. Hampson (ARPT).*

This undated image could be dated if we knew when the 3F 0-6-0T was renumbered to 47541. Alas we do not have that information to hand. Nevertheless, the tank engine has undergone a 'bit' of a spruce-up around the smokebox perhaps in readiness for the fitting of the new five-digit BR numberplate? This engine came new to Inverness as No.16624, the last, numerically, to grace the Highland lines. Shortly after receiving its BR number the 3F was transferred to Polmadie and their likes were never again to work north of Glasgow!

S.C. Crook (ARPT).

The main erecting shop of the adjacent locomotive works, known as Lochgorm, where, according to published records, forty-one of the Highland Railway locomotive fleet were actually built. I'm not sure how that figure corresponds with the total of locomotives operated by the Highland but one thing for sure is that all of the fleet were overhauled or repaired there. This undated view from the 1950s shows four Stanier Cl.5s and their respective tenders undergoing various intermediate level overhauls and repairs. Besides this shop, there were others where locomotives could be maintained up to Intermediate level but many of the service repairs which should have been tended to at the roundhouse shed were completed in here, a useful facility for 60A. Note that not a Highland engine was in sight, perhaps they had all gone by now! The locomotive works closed in 1959 to steam repairs after which it was converted for diesel locomotive use; it is still used today for railway business. *J.D. Mills, M. Halbert coll.* 23

It is easy to forget that the LNER, and the GNofSR before them, worked services into Inverness and for many decades their locomotives required servicing and stabling overnight. The practice continued into BR days so it was not unusual to find one of the former GNofSR 4-4-0s in town requiring a bit more attention than servicing. The D40 class 4-4-0s were basically 'all-rounders' and could work in from the east on passenger or freight trains. This is Keith's No.62268, a rather grotty specimen if I may say so, which has had some misfortune with a set of coupled wheels and was recorded on film languishing alongside the erecting shop (on the left) of the works at Lochgorm on an unknown date in the 1950s.   *J.D. Mills, M. Halbert coll.*

The tender-less D40 on the Inverness turntable with 'Pug' shed pilot No.56038 looking after its needs. It is unknown if No.62268 was en route to the workshop or was returning to the roundhouse after a successful conclusion to its dilemma, and was about to be coupled to its tender. For more information on the D40, why not try *Yeadon's Register of LNER Locomotives*, Vol.44, which is available from all good outlets or direct from this Publisher. Back to the 'Pug' note the BR wording atop the saddle tank.

J.D. Mills, M. Halbert coll.

Let's wind down the Inverness sequence with some nice moody views such as this from Tuesday evening, 1st July 1958. Ex-CR 3P No.54463 looks rather splendid whilst stabled in one of the outside stalls created when the roundhouse was refurbished and radically altered in the 1940s. The 4-4-0 is virtually ex-works and the side of the tender has one of those new but wrong facing BR crests – you know the ones: left is right, right is wrong – however, let's look past that little glitch and admire the locomotive which is coaled and ready for its next working to where? No.54463 was transferred to Inverness from Carstairs shortly after BR came into being. After steam was banished from the Highland lines it ended up at Polmadie where in December 1962 it was withdrawn.   *I.S.Jones (ARPT).*

Sunset for Inverness!? Well not quite but the sun is going down as it is now 1945hrs exactly on Friday 3rd August 1956. Stanier Cl.5 No.45366, one of Perth's rampaging horde stands like a sentry at the gates of the roundhouse. The '5' is not yet turned for home but being on one of the outside stalls will require use of the turntable to get out anyway and then! Once steam had vacated the roundhouse and the depot in August 1962, the building was at first left vacant but was later used for a short while by the diesels which had been part of the Inverness allocation since February 1960. Eventually the demolition gang moved in and that rather nice piece of architecture disguising the water tank was torn down. One wonders what kind of outcry there would be today if such a structure was even threatened! In the 1960s, and especially on the railway system of Britain, the authorities could and did get away with everything.

F.W. Hampson (ARPT).

Dingwall sub of 60A

Dingwall shed on an unknown date in BR days but probably very late 1950s as the doors have gone. Built entirely of timber, the shed was opened in 1870 to serve the junction of lines to Strome Ferry and later Kyle of Lochalsh (1897) and northwards to Wick and Thurso. The structure we see here is the original building which unusually for a wooden shed survived all that could be thrust upon it including the usual suspects in these parts; fire and tempest! The high pitched roof ensured that snow would not be a problem either. Although engine pits were provided inside the shed only that on the nearest road catered for outside preparation. The pair of wagons was gathered for two reasons, to take away the ash and clinker, and provide a platform for coaling the engines. A coaling stage being situated behind the photographer alongside the public road but using that platform would have required double handing of the coal; it was better to shovel directly from the wagon into the tenders and bunkers. Closure coincided with the gradual withdrawal of steam motive power and the introduction of diesels on the Highland lines and although it is difficult to pin point exactly when the shed was officially signed-off as not being required, the withdrawal of the Dingwall pilot in late 1961 would indicate disuse. *J.W. Armstrong (ARPT).*

The clear sunlight of an April morning in 1954 bathes ex-Caley 3P No.54458 standing outside Dingwall shed ready for work. The 4-4-0 was one of the Inverness lot and like all the rest of them took turns at the various sub-sheds in the Highlands. Before transferring to Inverness in November 1950, it was at Perth but came north initially to Wick in October 1950 before settling back at 60A. There would have been another locomotive here had we been early enough but the second engine, probably another ex-CR 4-4-0 or even a Stanier Class 5 would have left early to take up banking duties up Ravens Rock on the Kyle line. Note that the two outer doors of the shed are still in situ – just – at this time whereas the inner pair have disappeared; no doubt mangled by wind and moving locomotive. They probably ended up in fireboxes on Sunday's.   *C.J.B. Sanderson (ARPT).*

Dingwall shed on a Sunday morning in August 1957 with nearly a 'full house' of two pre-Grouping engines and a Class 5. No.54458 is once again resident and this was to be its final summer working at Dingwall or indeed anywhere because the scrap man called and in December the 3P was condemned. The other old-timer is ex-Caley 2P 0-4-4T No.55199 which had been allocated to Inverness virtually since Grouping, courtesy of the LMS; it was joined by sisters Nos.55227 and 55198 in September and November 1958 respectively. Another one of their kind was No.55216 which had been at Inverness since September 1952 and no doubt worked the Dingwall pilot on many occasions. Just before the shed closed what was probably the most unusual occupant took up station in July 1961 in the shape of 0-6-0 Pannier tank No.1649 which apparently became the last steam locomotive working north of Inverness.

C.J.B. Sanderson (ARPT).

Just over 63 miles from Dingwall is Kyle of Lochalsh, the most westerly point of the old Highland Railway. Reached in 1897, the port was created to replace Strome Ferry and offered a greater convenience for maritime traffic to the Western Isles. Whereas the passenger station and adjacent pier appeared to have plenty of room, the engine shed and its associated facilities had a somewhat restricted site where ordered discipline was necessary to service and stable the locomotives. This view captured on 14th June 1962 shows the shed and coal stage, along with part of the turntable, just a year after steam was banished from the line. The reason for the Stanier Class 5 appearing here is because it had hauled a joint SLS-RCTS rail tour to the terminus. No.44978 is just dropping back towards the station after using the still operational turntable. From opening, when this cutting and turntable pit was hewn out of the rock, a sequence for bringing engines on shed and getting them tucked-up was enacted with each arrival, and departure. Coming on shed, engines would run onto the turntable after stopping at the coaling bank; a water tank had been provided so that water could be taken on at the same time as coal. It was then the turn of the fire and ash pan to be cleaned and this was done outside the shed over a pit. Completed, the engine could be put into the shed; a second engine could be dealt with whilst fire cleaning was in progress. Getting off shed was the reverse procedure minus the need to turn or refuel. Without doubt the Kyle situation would make an interesting model. Note the old coaling bank platform which was disused (except for storing coal) long before steam was banished and was replaced during LMS days by a shelter over the wagon road. This gave the coalmen a semblance of cover during the passing of the ever present moisture laden westerlies' whilst they shovelled the coal directly into tenders from the wagons. Like Dingwall, double-handling at Kyle was a thing of the past. *Ian H. Hodgson (ARPT).* 31

The shed when fully operational on Monday 15th August 1960; nearest is Stanier Cl.5 No.45497 from Perth whilst No.45090 from Inverness stables at the side of the shed by necessity. Locating the wagon on the other shed road to receive the ash and clinker was in itself another shunting move which had to be thought about. The grounded coach body on the right (there were, at least two here) was one of the dormitories/mess rooms for visiting enginemen which was a daily occurrence.

Howard Foster.

Nearly a year has passed since the featured rail tour brought the Class 5 to Kyle of Lochalsh. It is now Saturday 11th May 1963 and some changes have taken place at the shed site. The place is still used to stable the Type 2 diesel motive power and the grounded coach bodies are still in situ but were they actually in use for visiting crews to overnight anymore? The engine shed roof is stripped of cladding whilst the shed is deserted and probably in the throes of slow demolition. There is no sign of a catastrophic fire which is supposed to have overtaken the place shortly after steam had vacated. With its now sun bleached timbers, the coal bank is intact as is the shelter with its single shaded light bulb. Note the water tank and that carefully stowed 'bag' waiting for the next customer; would there be one? *John Boyes (ARPT)*.

60B Aviemore

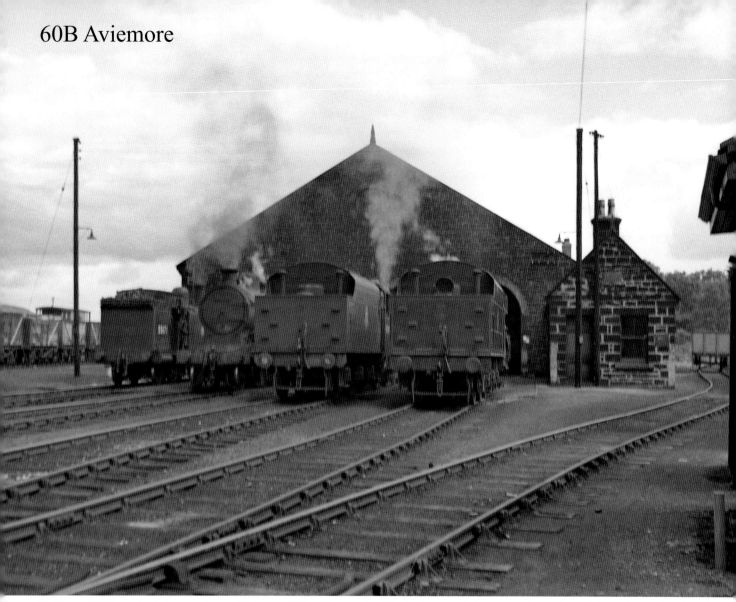

Full house! Well nearly. Aviemore shed on 4th August 1956 with a couple of '5s' and two ex-Caley engines in residence. Never a large allocation, 60B could boast anything from half a dozen to a dozen assorted engines throughout BR days but most were still of pre-Grouping types even in 1959. In 1935 ten engines made up the all-Highland allocation including 'Castles', 'Bens', and 'Lochs'. This shed was late in coming compared with most Highland establishments and didn't become operational until 1898. The design was the same as most of the others – why spoil a good thing when everything works! – those arches setting off the stone walls.

F.W. Hampson (ARPT).

The depot, as seen from a passing train, circa 1955!

J.D. Mills, M. Halbert coll. 35

Virtually the same aspect as the previous image, but now circa 1960! Again undated but the locomotives on view albeit with no numbers visible are a BR Std. Cl.2, an EE Type 1 Bo-Bo diesel, Cl.5, and a Fairburn Cl.4 tank. Now Cl.2 No.78052 was allocated November 1958 to July 1962; the EE Type 1 was new and during the first three months of 1960 Inverness received three new EE Type 1s, D8032 to D8034. The Cl.5 could have been anyone of a hundred or more but the Cl.4 No.42269 was the only one of its type resident and was allocated from May 1957 ex-Dalry Road to August 1961 when it transferred to Dumfries just as Aviemore shed was getting rid of the steam complement. So, to such up 1960 seems to be a reasonable time.

J.W. Armstrong (ARPT).

Yet another undated image of Aviemore! Now you could be forgiven in thinking that steam was long gone, and the diesels had taken over completely. But look around; stabled outside is one of the BRC&W Type 2s which became the mainstay of the Highland motive power; inside the shed is a BR Sulzer Type 2 peeping out of the No.1? road. The pit on No.2 road contains some burning embers of a fire clean-out whilst in the siding on the right of the shed is a stored Fairburn tank. The latter went in August 1961 just as the shed closed to steam. The first Type 2s of each class which came to Inverness to stay were D5338 which arrived on 27th February 1960 as part of the advance guard; D5114 came in April 1960 and was the first of the BR diesels which were also to serve the Highland lines well, D5115 to D5132 followed.   *K.H. Cockerill (ARPT).*

At some time in the past, former Highland Railway six-wheel, 20-ton brake van had been modified as a Tool Van for the Motive Power Dept. as their M-D294038. The lifting date was 23-8-41, whilst the paint date was 14-2-50. It was connected to the rest of the breakdown train so was obviously operational. The date when the image was recorded, 24th April 1955, was a Sunday. The roof is unusual with its lookouts projecting through the roof; the latter incidentally is clad in what appears to be non-slip matting. I wonder why?   *C.J.B. Sanderson (ARPT).*

Now this is BRC&W Type 2 Bo-Bo D5328 outside the shed at Aviemore on 25th May 1963 when steam had basically been evicted from the Highland lines as far south as Perth. Note the tablet catcher nicely stowed in the specially installed compartment in the cab side sheet (it mirrored the other side of the other end). The Inverness based members of the class were all given these recesses for working the mainly single-line routes of the former Highland Railway. Although they were delivered from the manufacturers with the recesses, the actual 'catching' apparatus was fitted by BR at either St Rollox or Lochgorm works. Besides those chosen members of this class of diesels, there were also a number of BR Derby built Sulzer Type 2s D5114 to D5132 so equipped with recesses and catchers and allocated to Inverness (delivered between April and September 1960), along with a few of the English Electric Type 1s – D8032 to D8034, D8031 joined them later; special provision for special circumstances! Also of note is the open cover – located just above and left of the BR crest – for the train heating boiler tank filler which has just been topped-off it seems. Other special fitments include the sloped cover over the air intake located above the front windows. It was in operational service where such requirements were found, the winters on the Highland lines being sometimes a bit more severe than those encountered in the Midlands of England for instance. D5328 was delivered new to Haymarket depot on 13th June 1959 and spent nearly two years there before 64B reluctantly gave it up to 60A.

C.J.B. Sanderson (ARPT).

Boat of Garten sub of 60B

For convenience sake, Boat of Garten engine shed became a sub of Aviemore when BR came into being. Prior to that event, the shed had been out on a limb from its distant parent at Kittybrewster. This undated illustration shows what appears to be a closed shed but only in the fact that there are no locomotives to be seen and the doors are shut but in reality the place was still operational; note the piles of ash and clinker and those two poles each rigged with a mechanism for coaling? Located at the junction of the GNofS line from Keith Junction and the Highland's old road to Inverness via Forres, the shed opened in August 1866 and was closed by BR in November 1958.

C.J.B. Sanderson (ARPT).

This is the shed on 10th August 1956 with an unidentified K2 taking on water. Standing on the raised coaling road is 'Ben' Class 2P 4-4-0 No.54398 BEN ALDER which had been withdrawn in February 1953 from Wick and which was now subject to a preservation appeal hence its transfer to this somewhat unusual facility. I should imagine that the engine was positioned on the raised coaling road to keep the shed roads clear but why would a locomotive listed for possible preservation be sent to a place where it could not be looked after or stored with a semblance of security. The 'Ben' was of course ex-Highland and had already been 'stored' for more than three years. The engine shed here was former LNER where the enginemen were still LNER (and possibly GNofSR too) some eight years into Nationalisation. What, if anything, did they care for a 'foreign' locomotive, and a dead one at that which was continually in the way of their day-to-day operations – not a good mix! Note the coaling poles still in situ.   *W.S.Sellar.*

The engine that never was: Ex-HR 2P 4-4-0 No.54398 BEN ALDER seeking shelter inside the shed at Boat of Garten on Saturday 22nd June 1957. Minus coupling rods, the 'Small Ben' remained here for another three years after the shed was closed, until 1961 when demolition of the building was imminent. The 4-4-0 was apparently whisked away to the south in the direction of Glasgow but once again the authorities quickly forgot about it and in the great cull taking place at that time the 'Ben' was broken up somewhere, with apologies all round once the deed was completed! Note the smoke ventilators; one at least looks the part whilst the nearer example appears to have given up. Now the sharp-eyed amongst you will note something different about the tender but you will have to wait until you reach Thurso to confirm your findings!   *C.J.B. Sanderson (ARPT).*

The shed on 7th August 1958 with J36 No.65297, another Keith engine, stabled by the old coaling bank with yet another six-coupled engine from Keith, ex Caley 3F No.57634. Integration of locomotive types was taking place but local customs and dyed-in-the-wool routines were still the order of the day as far as the enginemen were concerned. However, the coming of the diesels would change all that; or would it? *F.W. Hampson (ARPT).*

An undated but obviously BR period view (circa 1960) of Helmsdale shed with one unidentified occupant (we're not doing very well so far are we) stabled in the gloom of the building. This shed had what might be termed a typical Highland history – interesting, and somewhat disastrous at times with interludes of quiet. The building it will be noted was built from timber but so was the first shed here in 1871. That building, with its steep roof much like the covering at Dingwall, lasted until 1899 when it was listed for replacement but instead the HR in their usual parsimonious fashion took the shed to pieces, rearranged the main struts, replaced the rotten bits and rebuilt the second shed from what was essentially the old one! As luck would have it, the place survived numerous gales and bad winters and if only it had stood unscathed for a couple more years it would have been someone else's responsibility. However, in 1921 a gale finally took the shed to pieces and the HR had to fork out for a new building. Hey ho! The new shed was built in timber – why splash out on expensive materials when you had an inkling the place will not be your problem much longer? And so this is the shed as put together by the Highland. Although not the most attractive of buildings – that roof has something about it which isn't quite – engine shed! However, perhaps somebody connected with its design had been studying aviation and had the idea of a low curved roof and fast wind speeds seem to go together better than high pitched roofs! The curve will also help the snow accumulations slide. We have a winner. The shed survived for forty years at least until BR vacated it in 1961. Shunting the goods yard, which entailed running through the station and leaving the brake on the main line (luckily it was another of BR's less busy stations enabling shunting operations to go on uninterrupted between passenger workings), is 3F 0-6-0 No.57587 a long time resident of Helmsdale having moved to Inverness from Glasgow after WW2 but transferring to 60C in BR days.

Ken Groundwater (ARPT).

The last two Dornoch branch Pannier tanks Nos.1646 and 1649 were stored on the headshunt siding alongside the main line just north of the station, on the Up side. Both engines were treated in the manner befitting a locomotive that was still serviceable but redundant, temporarily or otherwise, with chimneys covered and bunkers emptied but with shed plates still fitted. Those 60C shed plates must have been quite rare with never more than six required for the allocation with a couple of spares in stores perhaps. Surely in the railwayana market of today those few examples – if they are still around – must be worth a lot more than say one of the 34A, or 81A plates. Anyway, the 60C plates were removed at some point prior to the engines departure. No.1646 arrived here in February 1957, transferred from Croes Newydd; sister 1649 came nearly eighteen months later in July 1958 courtesy of St Philips Marsh shed in Bristol. *Ken Groundwater (ARPT)*.

(opposite) One of the Dornoch branch tanks getting ready to come off shed at Helmsdale on Tuesday 27ᵗʰ April 1954; when not employed on the branch, the little 0-4-4Ts were given routine maintenance, boiler wash-outs and used on shunting jobs – they worked the Dornoch branch for a fortnight each time. No.55053 was due a major overhaul about this time and that event duly took place at St Rollox in Glasgow in 1955. Note the shed's coaling crane, just visible to the left.
R.F. Payne (ARPT).

Long term resident 3P No.54495 at the coaling bench. Although Helmsdale could boast a crane for hand coaling, the locomotives had to sit half-on the turntable if coal wagons were also alongside the bench, which invariably they were. The 4-4-0 looks smart enough and has just been partly cleaned, the gloss was not just an ex-works finish; allocated to Helmsdale for the whole of its BR career, No.54495 spent some of the war years working from Hurlford on the ex-G&SW whereas in earlier LMS days Perth South was its home. The date is 16ᵗʰ August 1960 and this ex-Caledonian Pickersgill 3P has not been near main works since its last 'General' in 1958 or late 57' because the tender wears one of the wrong-facing new BR crests which were 'outlawed' in 1958 by the College of Heralds. Note the 60ft articulated turntable which looks new but dated from 1948 – the Outdoor Machinery Department would have been pleased about this table; they kept things nice up here. However, when steam operations ceased in the Highlands our 3P was discarded like much else. Withdrawn in March 1962, No.54495 was sold for scrap to a yard near Glasgow.
H. Forster (ARPT). 47

Part of the shunting operations being performed in the first image of the Helmsdale sequence shows ex-CR 3F No.57587 positioning some important looking rolling stock whilst dragging a van on the headshunt (again we are undated but circa summer 1960 is looking good just after the Dornoch branch closed and luxuriant growth has got a grip of the local flora). The mail van appears to be an ancient HR example with little ridged roof windows and the ever present posting box next to the central entrance door (did any of you ever post a letter in one of those boxes?). The Gresley? vehicle appears to be a kitchen/restaurant car (or a buffet) which was probably working out its final days (if anyone knows the original of those vehicles we would be pleased to know what you know). The shed is vacant but it's probably a weekday when Helmsdale's half dozen resident's would be out earning their keep.

Ken Groundwater (ARPT).

Dornoch terminus on Friday 22nd June 1956 with the engine shed nearest; the passenger station centre background and the goods yard to the right. Note that the shed doors are closed, the summer season allowing the branch engine to stable outside; there was even room enough to allow the shunting locomotive space to position a mineral wagon on the coaling road without opening those doors. Of course winter was a different matter and the shed would then be utilised to the full. The Dornoch branch closed from Monday 13th June 1960 but the last train on the previous Saturday saw an end to the proceedings. The Pannier tanks which had taken on the branch work from the ex-HR engines, were laid-up initially at Helmsdale for storage before gradually making their way southwards towards oblivion, languishing at various sheds en route to Perth where one of them (unknown which) was recorded on 5th September 1962. Part of the mineral wagon seen in a later image being used as a platform, can be seen on the left. Finally, this view reveals, on the station platform, one of the various commodities once carried daily by the railways from the most obscure of stations – milk. Numerous churns are lined up awaiting the next train to The Mound, where they will await the next train to Inverness, where ....

C.J.B. Sanderson (ARPT).

In what appears to be an ex-works condition, No.55053 takes on water from the Dornoch tank on that Friday in late June 1956. Note that in this lined condition, the locomotive's number could not easily be 'shuffled' to the rear end so that now when the door was open only half of the number was visible. The water tank here was wooden in construction and resembles a wagon body; perhaps that was all it once was, a wagon body which had been caulked and sealed to make it watertight; certainly a cheaper solution than a cast iron tank? Only time would tell. Indeed it appears to have lasted the course because its services would not be required for much longer. The tank's base also looks to be a cheapskate affair, made of timber too with cladding to create storage space beneath.

C.J.B. Sanderson (ARPT).

No.55053 being coaled at Dornoch on that same Friday, 22nd June 1956! This close-up of the four-coupled tank reveals a rather dusty finish to the paintwork on this side of the engine. No coaling bench here and as for H&S, forget it, ingenuity is in play as the enginemen have lowered the wagon door so that it rests on the buffer of the tank. The door makes a superb platform from which to reach both the coal in the mineral wagon and the bunker of 55053 – two birds with one stone! Before it worked on the Dornoch branch, No.15053 was allocated to Wick and worked the Lybster branch until it closed in 1944. The lining on the front of the cab is novel and matches that on the tank fronts. *C.J.B. Sanderson (ARPT)*.

Not strictly an engine shed nor a junction with a shed but this view of No.55051 at The Mound assembling a train for the Dornoch branch allows us to see what these little four-coupled tanks were doing right up to their demise. Undated, the image shows the 0P wearing its first BR livery with the full lettering. The Highland Railway classified these locomotives as Unclassified, the LMS had them as 0P but BR had them initially as 0P and later as 1P although photographic evidence shows No.55053 in June 1956 and later with no markings on either side. Note the Pullman coach just peeping into the frame from the right; now what was that doing there?

R.F. Payne (ARPT).

No.55053 outside Dornoch shed during the early 1950s. It was obviously a summer because of the luxuriant growth of the trees and shrubbery in the background, and by the fact that enthusiasts tended not to venture north of Inverness except during the late spring and summer months. Note that the 0-4-4T is wearing a 1P classification on the front cab sidesheet above the 'A' and 'Y' of railways. It was this engine, overhauled and ready for a few more years of service, which took on the responsibility of working the branch after sister No.55051 failed a boiler exam during the summer of 1956. All went well until January 1957 when the 0-4-4T was withdrawn during the week ending Saturday 12th January. The cause of the premature end was a broken front axle which had nearly caused a derailment but thankfully the engine remained on the track whilst a wheel off the broken set preceded the locomotive for a short time before hitting a milepost. Luckily there were no casualties except to the ex-Highland tank which was the last operational HR locomotive on British Railways. A BR Standard Cl.2 2-6-0 (No.78052) was drafted in to Inverness as a replacement for No.55051 in November 1956 but from February it was reallocated to Helmsdale where it took up the mantle until the first of the WR Pannier tanks arrived at Helmsdale on 11th February. The Standard remained on the branch working alternating with No.1646 until No.1649 arrived in July 1958 when the 2-6-0 transferred to St Margarets but returned to Highland territory at Aviemore a few months later.

S.C. Crook (ARPT).

Tain sub of 60C

Captured on film from the Chapel Road bridge, just south of the passenger station, this was Tain engine shed on an unknown date in 1961 when it looked more like a goods shed than a stable for locomotives. The shed was apparently still open, on paper at least, and official closure did not take place until June 1962. The withdrawal of steam from the Inverness–Tain local services in June 1960 had seen the engines using this shed move away and soon afterwards rolling stock, mainly fitted vans, began to be stored at the shed. Opened in 1877, this building had replaced a wooden building erected in 1866 and which had burned down in typical Highland Railway 'fire & tempest' style in April 1877; the conflagration was apparently caused by a careless cleaner who was later dismissed! Motive power here was supplied by Helmsdale the parent shed 60C. 4-4-0s of various origins worked over the years but Stanier Cl.5s could be seen stabled after working from Inverness; a 60ft turntable in the goods yard north of the station enabled the 4-6-0s to turn. *J.W. Armstrong (ARPT).*

The rear aspect of Wick engine shed on 16th August 1960 after a slight shower. The 55ft diameter turntable was tucked away simply to keep the shed yard clear of such appliances which appear to get in the way at most other sheds in this part of the world. The two road building was opened for business in July 1874; double-ended and stone built with two through roads, the shed remained virtually unaltered to closure although the doors had by necessity been replaced numerous times. The latest door design used and fitted on the rear of the shed saw one door in full profile – as on both left side doors here – whilst the right side door had the upper curved section removed. It had obviously been worked out by somebody to be the best for what: smoke riddance; cutting down on sudden draughts or wind-shear? Anyway, modellers beware we'll be taking a close look at the doors on any BR period models of Wick engine shed we come across. The engine inside the shed is ex-Caley 3P No.54491 which came as a replacement for one of the Highland engines withdrawn in the early 1950s. Now what about that coal stack which has even managed to generate a small patch of grass on the left middle sector! It appears from the way the table is set and from the amount of vegetation on the left spur, that the right spur was the preferred route around the shed.

H. Forster (ARPT). 55

Three of the ex-CR 4-4-0s arrived at Wick during December 1952: 54459, 54491, and 54496. The latter had returned to Inverness the following May whilst 54459 was condemned in December 1954. However, Inverness had plenty of the type available and the Class 5s were always in attendance at Wick. In 1955 another ex-Caley veteran turned up in the shape of 3P No.54439 which had done a brief residency at Wick in late 1952. In August 1957 – yes another wet one – No.54439 is coaled up ready for an outing; it went for scrap in 1958. In May 1956 Stanier Cl.3 2-6-2T No.40150 was transferred from Aviemore to work the Thurso branch trains. It remained to the end then went south, initially to Inverness and then Perth where it was condemned in December 1962 and later sold for scrap. The last steam locomotive working at Wick was another ex-CR 3P, No.54495 which had come to replace sister No.54482 in October but in December its work was done and it left the diesels to get on with the job. *C.J.B. Sanderson (ARPT).*

'Ben' No.54399 BEN WYVIS stands out back at Wick on 25th April 1951. Besides the unorthodox chimney the tender has no emblem. Note also the three link coupling supplementing the screw coupling but where was the heating connection? Of the three Highland 2P 4-4-0s allocated to Wick in 1950: 54398, 54399, 54404, the latter was the first to go in October 1950, our subject here succumbed in May 1952 whilst controversial No.54398 kept going until February 1953.　　　*C.J.B. Sanderson (ARPT).*

Wick engine shed on Wednesday 6th August 1958 with Inverness Cl.5 No.45453 stabled alongside a very unusual visitor, Brush Type 2 D5511 which was conducting trials on the Highland lines and was in fact the first main-line diesel to visit these parts. As we all know, this particular class of diesel was not chosen to work the Highland lines but nevertheless the Brush had a good tour of Scottish lines during its secondment. In WW2 Wick was provided with a Stranraer type mechanical coaling plant and that was located just to the left of where the photographer was standing. Now Wick had never been coded by the LMS, Inverness being regarded as a garage depot to the main shed at Perth and therefore all the other ex-HR sheds were subs. BR changed that and from 1st January 1948 Wick essentially became 60D although it took some time for the code to take effect.

F.W. Hampson (ARPT).

Nearly in the same position as sister No.54399 but facing the other way, No.54398 stands at the rear of the shed in happier days, circa September 1951. Note that no doors were affixed to the shed and that the coal stack was in its infancy.   *S.C. Crook (ARPT).*

Thurso sub to 60D

Thurso engine shed stands on the right of this serene image of the terminus complete with a passenger station, goods yard and all the paraffle to rival Wick as 'Layout of the month'. Of course we mustn't forget that Thurso was the most northerly terminus, engine shed, goods yard, etc. The engine stabled outside the shed on this 25th April 1951, a Wednesday, was our old friend No.54398 which was allocated to Wick at that time and was therefore out-stationed to the sub shed. The 4-4-0 was to spend its final years working from Thurso and it might have been a decent idea to have kept the engine up here out of harm's way until constructive plans could have been made for its future. It must be early afternoon and activity at the station, along with the 'Ben' brewing up on shed would indicate a departure for the six mile run to Georgemas Junction is imminent. Then there is the little matter of the 147 mile run to Inverness but BEN ALDER will not be doing that today. More than likely one of the Stanier Class 5s will be the motive power. Happily, this scene is still available to photographers today albeit slightly contracted and altered. Even the train journey from Inverness is waiting for those with plenty of time to enjoy the scenery and spot the shed sites from the window.

C.J.B. Sanderson (ARPT).

No.54398 ready for the off on that Wednesday in April 1951. The engine is in good external condition and has a decent load of coal for the less than arduous duties it. Note the lack of a heating hose on the front connection, obviously with the turntable at Georgemas being available no tender-first running was envisaged. The brisk westerly wind is helping to keep the fire nice and hot. The tender itself lacks the BR emblem indicating non-availability when the 4-4-0 last went through shops; the tender remained that way to withdrawal and beyond. Perhaps the lack of a corporate identity.....?

C.J.B. Sanderson (ARPT).

Somewhere in Scotland! But where?! We have our suspicions but would like readers to confirm to us just where, and if possible when. Now perhaps it is my eyesight but the two gentlemen propelling the Royal Mail van on its circular journey appear to be pulling-pushing in the same direction? The notes with the negative read Thurso but that does not appear to be the case. It's a big table and was probably fitted with a vacuum tractor which was useless with this occupant aboard! Thurso's table was only 45ft in diameter with distinctive extension rails bolted on at both ends to extend it to 52ft. The table in the image isn't ex-LNER either. Oh yes, if the aforementioned gentlemen were not part of the motive power department then who were they? Here is a clue of sorts: That pit must have been difficult to dig! Answers, via the usual channels please, to the Publisher! We would like to hear from you and also please let us know where you purchased this album. We promise not to make a habit of illustrating red herrings in future albums.

K.H. Cockerill (ARPT).

Towards the end of steam at Thurso, with anonymous 3P No.54482 working the branch on this day; the date is 16th August 1960 and the 4-4-0 was officially allocated to Aviemore but that doesn't appear to be the case. For some reason the bolt heads on the smokebox door have been painted as have the figures on the numberplate, along with the centre boss on the opening handle. You look at the rest of the engine and then you ask yourself, why? The turntable here was taken out of use shortly after steam gave way to diesel workings on the branch in 1961 but a connection was put in to keep the shed available to any motive power requiring shelter. The diesel locomotives apparently preferred the station. Meanwhile, our intrepid 3P from Aviemore decided to stay at Wick until eventually evicted in 1961. Passing into private use, the shed building became a retail outlet until the late 1990s, the solid construction insisted by the HR taking it easily into its second century of occupation. *H. Forster (ARPT)*.

60E Forres

Forres engine shed on Thursday 10th July 1958 with that appearance afforded old buildings which have basically come to the end of the line although this establishment would see further use by steam locomotives for another ten months until May 1959, then a little longer by diesel locomotives. On this date most of the allocation (three 3P 4-4-0s, a 3F 0-6-0, and a couple of tank engines) was out working. Forres was the first of the BR-coded ex-HR depots to close to steam but once the diesels had settled in over the Highland lines, the rest soon followed; not that diesels spent much time here, because when they did the station precincts would be preferred for stabling and the shed was eventually demolished about a year after the official closure of May 1962, and a hundred years since being built. Coded 60E by BR, the shed had been coded by the LMS from 1935 when it became 29K under Perth, then 32C under Inverness.

Ian Falcus.

CR McIntosh '812' class 3F No.57620 was part of the Forres allocation on 10th July 1958 and is seen coupled to visiting Stanier Cl.5 No.45476 from Inverness. The 0-6-0 was the only one of its type allocated to 60E throughout the 1950s but on the impending closure of Forres, the 3F was transferred to Polmadie where....! Does anyone know what the H1 target board depicts? 3P No.54480 had the H4 version on the same day, whilst one of the Inverness 'Pugs' was carrying H16.
C. Campbell (ARPT).

Aviemore based '812' No.57597 had worked into Forres on Monday 23ʳᵈ April 1951 with a freight train and was waiting for a load to take back south. Shortly after this scene was recorded, the 0-6-0 transferred to Inverness. Pictures of pre-Grouping locomotives especially wearing the new BR numbers and coupled to tenders with LMS adorning the sides are no rarities. Whilst we are looking at the tender, just have gander at the size of those axleboxes! *C.J.B. Sanderson (ARPT).*

(opposite, top) Forres shed had a number of items of former passenger vehicles now in the employ of the Motive Power Department such as this ex-Highland 6-wheel passenger brake stabled in the yard on 28ᵗʰ May 1955. For all you coaching stock aficionados, its Departmental number was DM297293. It appears to be in good condition considering it was at least 32-years old. *F.W.Hampson (ARPT). (opposite, bottom)* Now we are spoiling you rolling stock fans with yet another Departmental vehicle in the shape of this former Glasgow & South Western 6-wheel brake at Forres shed on 23ʳᵈ April 1951. Numbered DM297291, it was in the employ of the Engineers Department, Inverness District as a Ballast van, whatever that was! *C.J.B. Sanderson (ARPT).*

BALLAST VAN
ENGINEERS DEP?
INVERNESS DIST
D M 297291

DM297293
MOTIVE POWER DEPT
FORRES.

Eleven years on and time, along with the weather, has not been kind to DM297291. The date is 15th June 1962 and the van, now labelled STAFF is apparently rotting in a siding near the engine shed; surely its days were numbered?

F.W. Hampson (ARPT).

Let's get back to some locomotives before the Title Description police drop us a line! Its 28th May 1955 again – not quite, only in the image – and Forres shed shows off one of its 3P ex-Caley 4-4-0s, No.54472 which, along with sisters 54471 and 54473, formed the backbone of the depot's fleet of passenger motive power from the mid-1950s up to closure. Our subject, which looks ready for a repaint, was transferred to 60E from Inverness in March 1953 as a replacement for sister No.54481 which was condemned in the summer. In the mid-LMS period and earlier, the allocation at Forres was not only larger but had more of a Highland flavour. In the summer of 1935 for instance eleven locomotives were 'on the books' of which ten were of pure Highland ancestry, odd-man-out was LMS 3F 0-6-0T No.16623 (47540) – another 3F tank, No.16415 (47332) was sub-shedded at Burghead on the Hopeman branch. Amongst the ex-HR lot was the last of the eight Drummond 4P 0-6-4 tanks (known at Forres as Banking Tanks), No.15300, which was employed banking the trains up the fifteen mile 1 in 75 slog to Dava summit on the 'old route' to Boat of Garten. When that tank was withdrawn in 1936 the banking turns became exclusively 4-4-0 tender engine property. Of the other ten at Forres in 1935, all were 4-4-0 tender engines made up of two 1896-built 'Lochs' Nos.14380 LOCH NESS and 14391 LOCH SHIN; six 'Small Bens' Nos.14398 BEN ALDER (where have we seen that before!), 14399 BEN WYVIS, 14400 BEN MORE, 14401 BEN VRACKIE, 14402 BEN ARMIN, 14406 BEN SLIOCH; and a solitary 'Large Ben' No.14422 BEN A'CHAORUINN. By the time of the Liberation of France, only two of the ex-HR 4-4-0s resided here, the Caley 4-4-0s began their slow take-over.

F.W. Hampson (ARPT).

70   More rain expected! A visitor from Inverness; 3P No.54484 graces the shed yard on Wednesday 31st July 1957.   *D. Fairley (ARPT).*

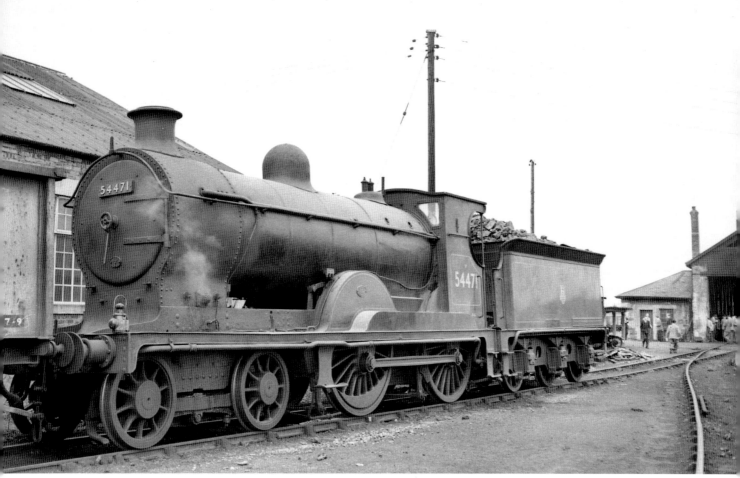

Resident No.54471 basks in the Highland sunshine on Saturday 16th May 1959 as a group of enthusiast's tour the depot for what was probably the final time as closure was imminent. We have touched on the subject before but once again it is worth a mention; the shed plates worn by the small band of engines allocated to these Highland sheds must be much sought after as very few were actually cast, the 60E batch probably never amounted to fifteen examples; and who took them off? No.54471 was withdrawn in October 1959 but where? Forres, Inverness, Perth?   *N.W. Skinner (ARPT).*

Let's give the last page over to this image of 'Loch' 2P No.14385 LOCH TAY which was the subject of attention for a group of RCTS members visiting Forres on Thursday 26th May 1949. There are a dozen gentlemen on and around the 4-4-0 but where they originated is unknown; was this group the genesis of those famous RCTS annual tours of Scottish engine sheds using motor coaches? The 2P was the last of its kind not only allocated to Forres but extant on BR, the following March would see the 4-4-0 withdrawn from Forres. Would such a locomotive be preserved today? I should imagine that doesn't even require an answer. However, in the years after WW2 when shortages were still commonplace and anything that was old-fashioned, dirty, and decrepit, especially worn-out machinery, everyone wanted new, clean, and quiet, no matter what it was. On that melancholy note, what of the Forres allocation in the immediate post-war period: Coming out of the hostilities the shed had five 4-4-0s of varying vintages, along with ex-CR 'Castle' 4-6-0 No.14678 GORDON CASTLE which had gone to that big shed in the sky, along with all eighteen of its classmates by 1946; another former CR engine, McIntosh 3F 0-6-0T No.16301 had taken over from the LMS Standard tank and was there to stay, at least for the period leading into the BR era; finally, three ex-Highland Drummond 0-6-0 tender engines, Nos.17696, 17698, and 17704 evened the balance but only one of them received its BR number – 57698 – neither of the others even reached Nationalisation. No.57698 was one of the last Highland engines in existence when it ended up at Hurlford shed, via a stint at Corkerhill, where it was condemned in December 1951.   *K.H. Cockerill (ARPT).*
Next stop – Aberdeen!